eBay Motors Money Machine

How I Make $500 a Week Selling Used Auto Parts on eBay

Copyright © 2014 by Master Mechanic

Table of Contents

Getting Started

After fifteen years of working as a mechanic for a local GM dealership the one thing I can tell you is cars are going to break down. The other thing I can tell you is people are always going to need replacement parts to fix them.

And that's where this guide comes in.

I'm going to show you how I make $500 a week (usually much more) selling used auto parts on eBay. And, the great thing is—it's something anybody can do, if you don't mind getting a little dirty or greasy.

What I'm going to show you doesn't require a fancy education or previous experience selling on eBay. You don't even really need to know anything about cars or car parts, but if you do—that's a big plus that can help you make even more money.

What got me started selling car parts was I had an old mustang I always planned to restore. Then I got married. We had a kid, and the car sat there in the driveway gathering dust and complaints from the neighbors about it being an eyesore.

Finally, I had enough and decided I'd try to sell it on Craigslist, but I didn't get any takers. I called the scrapyard. They offered me one hundred bucks. I was pretty sure a few of the parts alone were worth more than that.

Several days later I got this crazy idea. What if I part it out on eBay? I was sure to get more than $100.

Over the next three weeks I pulled every part I could off of that car—shift knobs, shifter arm, distributor, glove box door, hood emblem, and window crank handle. You name a part, I put it up for sale, and the funny thing is they sold.

Someone paid me $33.00 for a window crank, $25.00 for the Mustang horse emblem, and $25.00 for the owner's manual.

It was nuts! People emailed to ask if I had this or that part left. When I got their emails I'd head back out to the car with my wrench and screw driver to yank it out for them. I'd come back in the house and list the part on eBay for the agreed upon price.

After three weeks I'd sold close to $700 in parts from a car the junkyard offered a hundred bucks for.

All I could think was—I need another car.

That's when my brother-in-law popped into my head. He had an old Blazer. He was always saying he needed to get rid of it. I offered to take it off his hands for fifty bucks, and he said okay.

By this time I was pretty much hooked.

The Blazer parts sold for close to $1000. I picked up a few more Junkers on Craigslist and made a couple dollars on them.

The money was good, but it was just too much work. I told myself there had to be an easier way—one that didn't take so much time, effort, or hard work.

That's what I'm going to cover next—how to get all of the used car parts you want without the hassle of having to buy the entire car and strip it down—without having to get all greasy and dirty.

The profit is a little slimmer than when you harvest the parts yourself, but you can make it up in volume.

Let's get started…

Read this first

Like I said in the beginning of this book, the great thing about this business is cars are always going to break down and people are always going to need parts to fix them. It doesn't matter if it's a water pump for a 1988 Firebird or a door handle latch for a 2008 Malibu, somewhere somebody is looking for that part.

If you can help them get the part they need for less money all of a sudden you become their hero and have the opportunity to make more sales.

The cool thing about selling auto parts is when somebody goes on eBay to look for a part you can damn well be certain there's something wrong with their car. They're gonna buy that part. It's just a matter of who they're going to buy it from.

It's not like when a collector goes cruising around eBay looking for a book, a baseball card, or whatever. They generally don't need those items today to solve a problem. They have plenty of time to shop around first and find the exact one they're looking for at the price they want to pay.

When people are looking for a car part, chances are they need it yesterday—or their car isn't going anywhere.

Many of your potential customers are suffering from sticker shock. The last time they replaced an alternator was ten or twenty years ago. Back then you could pick up a rebuilt alternator for $25 or $35. Today they're computerized and sell for $400 or $500. Because of this customers are willing to shell out $125 for a used one if it'll save them a little green. The only problem is their local scrapyard doesn't have one available, so they hop onto eBay and hope they can find the part they need.

Ka-ching! That's a stack of twenty dollar bills in your pocket.

Keep that fact in mind as you get started in this business. Everyone who looks at your listing is there for just one reason. They have a problem. They need your part to get their car fixed and back on the road.

The easier you make it for them to do business with you the more sales you're going to make.

This means –

1. You need to offer a large selection of parts

2. You need to set a competitive price

3. You need to excel at customer service

4. You need to offer fast shipping

Let's take a minute to explore each component in more detail, and how it plays into your winning strategy for selling on eBay.

You need to offer a large selection of parts. This one is a no brainer. If you only offer ten or twenty parts you're not going to make as many sales as you would if you offer one hundred or one thousand parts.

Like everything else, selling on eBay is a numbers game. If you only offer ten parts you're catering to a small audience and less likely to make a sale. The more parts you offer for sale, the more potential buyers you're going to reach.

As a result, you're going to make more sales.

You need to offer a competitive price. If you price your parts too high, fewer people are going to look at you're listings because they feel you're over-priced. If you price your parts too low, people are going to wonder if there's something wrong with them. As a result, you're only going to get the lowball business.

I decided early on I was going to compete head on. Whenever possible I price my items just under the lowest realistic price. Let's say I'm going to sell a windshield washer pump. I'll do a quick search on eBay to see how many are for sale, and how much sellers are asking. Normally I disregard the highest and lowest prices. I look at what the majority of items are selling for and try to set my price a few dollars cheaper. Whether I can do it or not depends upon my margins.

You need to offer great customer service. If customers email you with questions you need to answer them as quickly as possible. When I ran leads for my car dealership they expected us to respond within ten minutes during business hours. After business hours we had an auto-responder set up with answers to basic questions. The next day we fired off an initial email to everyone within an hour of opening. The goal was to get back to the customer as quick as possible before another dealership snagged them.

You want to do the same thing. Answer every email as quick as possible. Respond directly to the customer's questions. Take a few moments to build a relationship. Talk about your great selection of parts, your superfast shipping, or your awesome return policy. Your goal should be to make customers feel good about doing business with you.

You need to offer fast shipping. What you need to keep in mind is your customers are anxious to get their cars working and back on the road. That means you need to ship all orders as quickly as possible. Offer a standard shipping option for buyers who want to save some money and don't mind waiting a little longer for their items to be delivered. Offer a quick shipping (or priority) option for customers who want their item sooner (normally within one to three days). And, make sure to offer a super-fast delivery option (express mail) for customers who need it now.

My suggestion is to offer free standard shipping on your bestselling items. Free standard shipping will bring more buyers to your item page. With a little luck some of these

lookers will take a peek at the other items you're selling, and

buy more items from you.

Where to Get Your Parts

Hands down, the best place to source the parts you're going to resell on eBay is from local salvage yards.

Most communities have at least one auto salvage yard (junk yard), some have two or three. If you're not familiar with them check your phone directory, or run an online search.

After you locate a few salvage yards I'd suggest a personal visit. You don't have to talk with anyone this time around, it's more of a fact finding mission. Familiarize yourself with the business.

Before you walk in the door make a quick note of the hours (they're usually posted on the door). Many salvage yards also have signs explaining their return policies, discounts, etc. Some yards give a 10% senior discount if you're over 55. Others have special discount days—save 15% on Mondays. Make a note of any specials that might apply to you. It's a great way to increase your profit margin.

Most of the salvage yards I've dealt with have a similar setup. There's a bar running across the back wall where they have five or six work stations setup. When you first walk in the door you see a display of used tires, custom rims, etc. Over to one side of the showroom they have three or four display cases loaded with car stereos, DVD players, fuzz busters, etc. On the wall opposite that they have shelves loaded with all sorts of small parts, owner's manuals, and other goodies.

If you're handy with tools and know a little bit about cars find out if they offer "you pull it specials." Many salvage yards give you free reign to explore the yard and pull the parts you need. I've seen a large variety of pricing at "you pull apart yards." Some charge a flat fee of $20 or $25 for most parts.

Other yards have a specific price for each part, so if you don't see a sign, ask how it works.

Find out if they have an online parts list. Some salvage yards have an online list of parts and prices; others make you call a salesman to get a price. Most yards work with partner shops so if they don't have a part you want, they can search another yard's inventory and get it for you. In most cases there's an extra fee for this service. In my area it's $25.00 plus shipping.

Make sure to investigate all of the scrapyards in your area. They don't know it yet, but these guys are going to be your business partners. They're going to supply the fuel for your business success. So whenever you come into contact with one of their people you want to treat them right.

After you've been at this for a couple of months and have thirty or forty purchases under your belt it's time to talk with the manager. Don't be pushy or argumentative.

Explain to him a little bit about what you do. Make sure to let him know you're a good customer. Show him your stack of receipts if he needs proof.

Help him to understand that you've spent thousands of dollars there over the last few months, and you expect to spend even more over the upcoming year. Ask him if his company offers a trade discount. Some salvage yards have given me a 10% discount, some 25%, and some none. You never know until you ask.

. . . .

Another great place to pick up small parts and accessories is Wal-Mart, Target, Western Auto, and local hardware stores. Most of these businesses update their inventory every few months or at the end of every season.

I've found lots of great items I can pack away in my eBay store to pick up extra profits.

Here's what I look for –

- **CD cases**. Stores are constantly changing the style of CD cases they stock. Often times I can pick up a case that originally sold for $10 or $20 for just a dollar or two. I put them in my eBay store and sell four or five of them a month.

- **Cords and adapters**. What I'm talking about here is all of those strange cords you use to attach your iPod or cell phone to your stereo. Stores get overstocked on these or they change suppliers, and next thing you know these items end up in the close out bin. I normally pick them up for $1 and sell them for $5 or $10.

- **Cell phone cases**. Cell phone cases come and go. When stores are closing them out I look for something unique—sports teams, local products or events. Another steady seller is any case made of leather. They aren't fast sellers, but most times I pick up an extra fifty bucks a month selling phone cases and skins.

- **Spark plugs / filters / etc**. If the price is right, I pick up a bunch of these and group them together in ten or twenty dollar lots. They usually sell pretty quickly.

Keep your eye on the clearance bins. They're easily worth another few hundred dollars a month in profits.

. . . .

Craigslist is another great source for additional inventory.

I check the auto parts section at least two or three times a week. I'm look for the ads labeled "gotta go" or "must sell quickly." Most of these guys are motivated sellers and are willing to work with you on price.

I've scored some great deals on rims, radiators, and other parts by buying inventory from Craigslist sellers.

What Should I Buy

There are so many parts available, how do I decide what to buy?

That's the question every eBay seller turns over in their mind every day. There are millions of items out there that you can sell, but which ones are going to sell the fastest—for the best profit?

I don't have all the answers.

What I'm going to try to tell you here is how I choose the parts I sell.

I rely on the advanced search tool to determine which items to stock in my eBay store. It shows all the parts eBay buyers have purchased in the last thirty days—how much they paid for them, what price the item started at, and what type of listing it sold from.

This way there's no guesswork involved. Whether I sink five dollars or fifty dollars into a part I want to know there's a ready buyer out there looking for it.

Here's what you do.

If you've never used eBay's advanced search tool before, it's located at the top of the eBay page. Look for the search bar at the top of the page. To the far right you'll see a blue button that says search. Next to it you'll see the word "advanced." Select it.

Enter the keywords you want to search on. Normally I start with a general term "Ford Taurus parts." In the <in this category> drop down box I select <eBay Motors>. Below that in the <Search Including> section I check off <Completed Searches>. If it shows too many selections change your search to <sold>, so only sold items are shown.

Further down the page in the <Condition> section I check off <used>. After this you can scroll down to the bottom of the page and choose search.

The search results you're shown are for completed items. The listings shown in green are ones that closed successfully or sold. These are the only ones that matter. They show actual items that sold, and how much the items sold for.

The items listed in red are items that were listed but closed unsuccessfully, or in other words didn't sell. Be sure to look these over closely. They'll give you a good idea of what's not selling now. Losing auctions also show you what's not working price wise.

What I look for is parts that sold several times in the last thirty days. I make a note of the part name, the part number, the year and model of the car it is for, the high and low selling price, and four of the midrange selling prices. I also make a note about how it sold: auction, or fixed price.

I generally build a list of fifty or one hundred parts with a decent sales history. After I've finished my list I plug all of the information into an Excel spreadsheet.

My spreadsheet looks something like this going across the top…

- 1997

- Ford Taurus

- 3.0 Liter OHV Fuel injectors

- $129.99

- $99.99

- $105.99

- $103.97

- Auction / Buy-it-now

Next I crunch the numbers. From my research I know the low selling price is $99.99 and the high selling price is $129.99. The average selling price is $109.99. We can determine a more realistic selling price if we eliminate the $129.99 sale. That means the fuel injectors should sell for $103.32.

If my cost is $70.00 I'd price them between $97.00 and $99.99, which would give me a competitive price. Another option would be to price them at $103.99 with free priority shipping. This is especially effective if other sellers are charging $9.99 or some other ridiculous number for shipping.

We're not done quite yet.

You need to add a few more lines to your spreadsheet. Add one for the item cost (what you paid for it), add a line for eBay fees, add a line for PayPal fees, add a line for expected shipping costs, a line for your projected selling price, and add a line for your profit.

It sounds like a lot of work, but if you're in this to make money you've got to know the numbers work for each part you intend to sell.

The next step is to check the scrap yard's prices for the items you have on your list. If the yard has their prices online you can fill your spreadsheet in quickly. If you have to call for prices, I'd suggest asking for no more than five per call. Salvage yards are busy and you're going to try their patience if you force them to price fifty items all at once.

Once your list is done pick the top ten most profitable items, and list those. Keep updating your list and selecting new items. As one item sells choose another item and get it listed for sale.

Over time your business will grow and you will get better at picking winning items to resell.

eBay Listings 101

eBay has several ways to sell your items—auction, buy-it-now, or classified.

Auction listings are just like they sound. You place your item on the eBay site and sellers bid for it. The buyer who makes the highest bid wins the item. To supercharge their listings sellers can add a feature called buy-it-now. When you use buy-it-now you set two prices—a starting price, and a buy-it-now price where buyers can stop the bidding and buy the item now.

Fixed Price listings are just like going into your local Wal-Mart or Target store. Sellers set a price on their items. If buyers want your item they click the Buy-it-now button and it's theirs. eBay has an option called best offer to help buyers sell more items. With best offer sellers set a price on the item they are selling, and select an option that allows potential buyers to offer a lower price.

When I use best offer I set my price from 25 % to 50% higher than I normally would. If I'm lucky someone snaps it up at the higher price and I make a few extra bucks. What usually happens is someone makes an offer for 50% to 75% of my selling price. After a little negotiating we settle on a price that works for both of us.

Classified listings are used to advertise services such as real estate, specialty advertising, or book editing. The advantage to using classified listings is you can include contact information such as your phone number or email address. They're really not so helpful for selling auto parts.

What's the best listing type?

Whatever makes the sale? That's the easy answer. It really comes down to how long you've been selling on eBay and how many items you have listed for sale.

If you're a new seller eBay is going to place restrictions on your account. You'll probably be able to list between ten and twenty-five items per month. As you sell more items and receive good feedback eBay will raise your listing limits.

Think of it as a process. You have to prove yourself each step of the way. Keep making sales, and continue taking care of your customers. Each happy customer will help you level up and be able to list and sell more items.

A Few Words about Fees

Selling on eBay isn't free. Large sellers pay thousands of dollars every month for the privilege of selling on eBay.

Your goal as a seller is to keep your seller fees as low as possible. To do this you need to understand eBay's fee structure, as well as the fees you are charged by any third party service providers.

As a new seller eBay gives you fifty free listings per month. Currently they only let you use these for auction style listings. That means you can run your listings for one, three, five, or seven days. You can extend the listing to ten days for an additional fee.

As you sell more items, you're going to want to explore having an eBay store.

eBay has three different levels of eBay stores—Basic, Premium, and Anchor. The monthly fees for an eBay store range from $19.99 to $199.99. Discounts are available if you purchase a yearly subscription.

Basic store subscribers receive 150 free listings, Premium store subscribers receive 500 free listings, and Anchor store subscribers receive 2500 free listings. Anchor store subscribers also receive free basic listings on eBay's international sites to help turbo charge their sales.

When you first start out you don't need an eBay store. Over time as you grow and start increasing your listings an eBay store will help you lower your fees while at the same time giving you a place to feature all of your item listings in one place. An eBay store is a great way to encourage add on sales, and to build repeat customers.

All of the fees we've talked about so far are called store fees or insertion fees. You pay these fees to list your items for sale on eBay.

eBay also charges a final value fee when your item sells. In the auto parts category final value fees are 10% of what your item sells for (including shipping charges). As an example, if you sell a part for $20.00 plus $5.00 for shipping, your eBay final value fee would be $2.50.

You also pay roughly 3% in merchant service fees to PayPal for each item you sell where you receive a payment through PayPal. As a result your total eBay and PayPal fees on an item that sells for $25.00 are $3.25.

Every time you list an item for sale on eBay you need to keep the fees in mind and do a quick calculation to make sure you've priced your item high enough to cover all of your costs, fees, and a profit for yourself.

If the math doesn't work, mark the price up if you can. If not, take your lumps, and look at it as a lesson learned not to sell that item again.

Listing Your First Items

Listing items for sale on eBay seems hard at first, but after you've listed you're first few items you'll be going at it like a pro.

There are five elements to a good listing.

1. Title

2. Pictures

3. Description

4. Price

5. Shipping

If you can nail these five items you'll be more successful selling on eBay.

Title. Your title does a lot more than tell people what you're selling. It also acts as the search keywords for what you're selling.

Think of it this way. When you search for information on Google you enter keywords that help the search engine discover what you're looking for. The words you include in your auction title are the keywords eBay will use to help people find what you're selling.

When you write your title you want to include as many relevant keywords as possible—part name, part number, year, model, make of car, other vehicles it will work on, free shipping, fast shipping, rebuilt, and warranty.

The above is just a partial list, but if gives you a good idea of the info buyers are searching for.

Here are a few great titles I discovered on eBay Motors –

- 1964-1988 GM door striker – Torx Head GM #20151275 (fits 1983 Camaro)
- 1982-1992 Chevrolet Camaro / Pontiac Firebird headliner with T-Tops – black (fits – 1983 Camaro)

- 1970-1989 GM Windshield Washer Pump – white head, 2nd design (fits: 1981-1989 Camaro)

Notice each one of them gives the year, cars the part works for, color, etc.

Pictures. Every item you sell needs big bold pictures. They need to be close up and give a good view of the item you're selling from several different angles.

If the item you're selling has any damage, dings, bangs, or scrapes, be sure to mention them in the description, and also to show close up photos of the affected areas.

Pictures can be taken with your cell phone camera or from a good digital camera. Be sure to take them at medium or high resolution for the best results. eBay requires all photos to be a minimum of 500 pixels on the longest side. They recommend 1600 pixel on the longest end for best results when buyers are looking at blown up images of your pictures.

One of your first investments should be a light-box. They start at $29.99 on eBay. The advantage is a light-box comes with a tripod for your camera, flood lights to provide backlighting for your item, and several choices of backdrop colors. Using a light-box will give your photos a more professional image and help you sell more items.

Description. A good description is short and to the point. It gives all of the relevant details about your item, lists any damage, and tells potential buyers a little more about you and why they should buy from you rather than one of your competitors.

Here's a great description I found on eBay Motors.

OEM ENGINE COMPUTER FITTING

PART NUMBER: 1226026

Also works with:

. PONTIAC 2000 1983 Elec Cont Unit (ECU); 4-121 (2.0L)

. CHEVROLET CAMARO 1983 Elec Cont Unit (ECU); 8-305 (5.0L), EFI

. CHEVROLET CAVALIER 1983 Elec Cont Unit (ECU)

. CADILLAC CIMARRON 1983 Elec Cont Unit (ECU)

. CHEVROLET CORVETTE 1984 Elec Cont Unit (ECU); AT

. PONTIAC FIREBIRD 1983 Elec Cont Unit (ECU); 8-305 (5.0L), EFI

. OLDSMOBILE FIRENZA 1983 Elec Cont Unit (ECU); 4-121 (2.0L)

. BUICK SKYHAWK 1983 Elec Cont Unit (ECU); 4-121 (2.0L)

ALL ITEMS TESTED AND GUARANTEED TO WORK LIKE NEW

It's a good description it lists the part, the vehicles it's compatible with, and mentions that it's tested and guaranteed to work. If you can do this in all of your items you'll make more sales.

Price. You can do everything else right, but if you get the price long—it's no sale.

Pricing is part art, and part science. I've already talked a little bit about my pricing strategy. I don't offer the lowest price or the highest price; instead I aim to be competitive. I try to price my items a few dollars under the average selling price for that part. Sometimes I offer free standard or priority shipping. It depends on what other sellers of that part are doing.

I do my best to find a competitive advantage for my item—be it price, shipping, or if the money's not there I try to do it by writing a better description or by including better pictures.

The key takeaway is I do whatever I can to make my listing stand out in the buyers mind.

Shipping. Shipping is all about offering your customers choices so they can receive the items they purchased as quickly as they want. For price conscious customers I offer free or low priced shipping. If a customer needs their item quicker, I offer a variety of fast shipping options. For a price upgrade they can choose priority mail or next day shipping.

The key to winning the shipping game is to offer a wide variety of choices, and let the buyer decide what fits their budget and time frame.

Final Wrap up

Selling used auto parts on eBay is a great way to make extra money.

It's not a get rich quick scheme. You aren't going to make a million dollars overnight. But if you're willing to put the time and effort into it you can make some good money. I went from zero to five hundred dollars in my first month, and things just kept going up from there.

Keep in mind it doesn't always work like that. The first items I sold were virtually free because the parts I sold came from a car I already owned. I was just as lucky with my second purchase. I picked up an old Blazer from my brother-in-law for fifty bucks.

Most people aren't going to be that fortunate. You're going to have to buy your parts from the salvage yard and make a smaller profit.

How much money you eventually make in this business is going to depend on how well you pick the items you choose to sell on eBay, and how well you take care of your customers.

Your goal the first year shouldn't be to make money. It should be to build the number of items for sale in your inventory. No matter what you do, you need to keep reinvesting at least fifty percent of your profits back into your business.

As you level up and prove to eBay that you're able to provide good customer service and deliver the items you're selling, they will eventually lift all of the limits on your seller account. When that happens you'll be able to build the business you want.

Always keep the end goal in mind and you'll be successful.

www.ingramcontent.com/pod-product-compliance
Lightning Source LLC
Chambersburg PA
CBHW021416170526
45164CB00002B/675